Sugar Fix

Also by Kory Wells

Heaven Was the Moon (chapbook)

Sugar Fix

Kory Wells

Terrapin Books

© 2019 by Kory Wells
Printed in the United States of America
All rights reserved.
No part of this book may be reproduced in any manner, except for brief quotations embodied in critical articles or reviews.

Terrapin Books
4 Midvale Avenue
West Caldwell, NJ 07006

www.terrapinbooks.com

ISBN: 978-1-947896-21-5
LCCN: 2019940779

First Edition

Cover art by Janet Hill
Twelve Days at the Penny Fontaine Hotel. Day Six
oil on canvas

for Mike

&

for all the story makers,
especially my grandmothers
known and unknown

Levida Tennessee Bingham Lee Gilbreath
1926-1998

Dorothy Jones Cantrell
1672-1755

Contents

Dear Reader   7

Chocolate, Chocolate, Chocolate
   Untold Story   11
   He drove a four-door Chevy, nothing sexy,
     but I'd been thinking of his mouth for weeks   13
   Still Won't Marry   15
   Letter to a Distant Cousin, Star of Stage and Screen   16
   Cenotaph   19
   On This Uncertain Earth   22
   You Are Not Who You Thought You Were   24

Layers of Rich Wonder
   As the Story Goes   29
   Getaway   31
   Postcards from the Cookie Jar   33
   Mahaley Explains   34
   Parable of the Pale Girl   35
   Some Notes and Three Word Problems
     on Red Velvet Cake   36

The Last Wedge of Apple Pie
   In This Bright Land   43
   Due to Chronic Inflammation   46
   "All Things Are a Darkness"   48
   They Taught Us in School to Sing
     of the Huddled Masses   51
   On the Importance of Literature   53
   Redoubt   54
   My Zinnias Grow Like Good Intentions   58

The Biggest Buttercream Rose
   Unlike Emily's   61
   I confess I've never been completely satisfied   62

"We Climb onto the Motorcycle of Sleep"	64
Questions from the Women for Dorothy, Wife of Richard Cantrell, Before the Grand Jury for Masking in Men's Clothes and Dancing at Nine O'Clock at Night, 1703	66
Her First Husband Was a Carpenter	69

Salve of Spun Honey

We're Young and This Is the Beginning	73
The Assistant Marshal Makes an Error in Judgment	75
With a Thousand-Tongued Hunger	77
Between Past and Present I Never Moved So Freely	79
"Let Us Suffer Our Radiance"	82
Fall Sanctuary	84
In the Secret Hour of Life's Midday	85

As I Already Said, Sugar

When the Watched Pot Boils	89
There's a God of False Starts and Tragic Mistakes	91
This Relic	93
Love Me Anyway	96
Voice	98
We Come Undone	100
So Long to the Good Old Moon	102

Acknowledgments	105
About the Author	109

*If you tell this story, say there was sweetness and wind;
that what fell fell like handfuls of stars—no, like handfuls of sugar.*
—Cecilia Woloch

It takes more than one story to tell a story.
—Michael E. Williams

Dear Reader

It's true that when
you're near I want

to kiss your cheek,
stroke my thumb

across your lips,
brush away

the pretense
of a crumb;

it's true I want to
invite you to paradise.

Or coffee and chocolates.
Or beneath the covers

of my bed. Yes,
I'm more tease

than temptress.
Truth is,

I'm simply lovesick
on possibility

alone, lovesick
for the intimate,

the tender, this sense
of you and me.

Think of us—
a cozy room,

an amber bowl
of light, a sprinkle

of sugar across
the clear night sky.

Would that not be
safe and true as

the stars? Isn't that
what we long for?

What I want for us
is this—a warm and quiet

place, and time enough.
Words. Breath. Turn

after turn of page. Rhythm
rising in our blood,

insistent as the moon,
round as our hopeful mouths.

Chocolate, Chocolate, Chocolate

Untold Story

She was religious   about reading aloud—
    Ann Landers' advice in the *Free Press*
      Jello salad recipes in *Good Housekeeping*
        letters and postcards from cousins
and one odd relation   all the way in Australia.

    But neither of us ever   said a word about
the *National Enquirer*
    which she'd pick up in the Winn Dixie checkout
      next to the gum and chocolate bars
  as if it were essential   as milk and sugar.

Back from the grocery
    on a summer afternoon
  she'd start supper
      and I'd slip away
  to the over-warm sanctuary
      of her modest living room:
    thin floral carpet   knotty pine walls
    and a nubby mauve sofa where I—
        a sensitive and impressionable child—
  would spread the tabloid
and kneel before it

    to absorb   cover to cover
      and back again
        until my knees ached
the gospel of my disbelief:
    a moon-landing hoax
  an alien abduction   a two-headed

            motherless kitten nursing
         a domesticated squirrel
and of course the secret
              lives of stars.

What is it that makes us want to swallow
   a story whole?   To think
      only one version can be true?

We were not   true disciples
  but my grandmother   tended the altar of
        narrative possibilities
    this woman with an eighth-grade education
        who I never saw   reading a book.

He drove a four-door Chevy, nothing sexy, but I'd been thinking of his mouth for weeks

when he finally called me up
and asked if I'd like to get
some ice cream.

I was full from supper and my
thighs sure didn't need it, but
I've never struggled with

priorities. That Dairy Queen
had gone downhill even then—
bright red logo faded like a movie star
who's kissed away all her lipstick—
but it still had a drive-in, and he
knew how I was about nostalgia

and sugar. This is how a place
became our song. We parked
under the sun-bleached canopy
and I leaned over him
pretending to read the menu.
Then at his rolled-down window
we confessed our desires
more or less into thin air,
which now that I think about it
sounds a little like church
and believe you me
I'd been praying about him.
How I wanted him,
how if I couldn't have him,

I wanted to be free
of want. Do you get that way
sometimes? Where all
you can think about is
chocolate, chocolate, chocolate,
or in my case man, man,
that man. The bench seat
of his Chevy became a pew,
the space between us palpable
as the early summer humidity.

I kept telling myself
it's just an ice cream,
but even then I knew
love is a kind of ruin.
When those cones arrived
so thick and voluptuous,
I almost blushed to open my mouth
before him, expose my eager tongue.

Still Won't Marry

> *Angeline the baker, age of forty-three,*
> *I feed her sugar candy, but she still won't marry me.*
> *—Traditional Appalachian song "Angeline the Baker"*

That man's professed his love for me for years,
but candy's all he's good for, sticky paper
bag each time he comes. Like I don't labor
over food all day, flour dust in every breath,
kneading dough 'til my sore knuckles swell.
He says a little taste of sugar will cure
my weary back, my aching shoulders, my
singed arms. Like I don't know what a man wants.

He wants to lean so close he'll smell vanilla
dabbed behind my ear. He wants to taste
my scent. Like I don't know what happens next:
The bed a pleasure too short. Babies. Chores.
His wants ahead of mine. Come night I dream
of water thick with sugar, simmering.

Letter to a Distant Cousin,
Star of Stage and Screen

       —after Life *magazine photos of Gypsy Rose Lee*
       at the Memphis Cotton Carnival, 1949

Dear Miss Lee,
I once thought we might be kin.

       Combing my genealogy for you,
I've found carpenters, farmers, generals, scores
of documented men, the women nothing
more than a headcount. I'm from a long line
of Lees myself, and it would shake the family tree
to have you studding it like some ripe, exotic fruit.
Although I've learned Lee's not your real name,

I like thinking of you as Cousin.

       With your act at the fair,
who'd want to gape at the bearded lady?
I've never seen anyone look so elegant as you
eating a hot dog. In street clothes, no less.
So self-possessed, in your mirrored dressing room,
bulky typewriter atop thigh-high fishnets.
And your name in lights, on such a large sign?
The sight gives me a thrill, and I'm not even you.

Gypsy. The word alone spangles

       my imagination, all those long letters
looping across the line of propriety: Gypsy
nip-of-morning-brandy tipsy, twirl-by-campfire
licking hips   lips   lipstick   trick   Hovick—

Dear Louise Hovick,
                    When you spoke to yourself
in the mirror, *You are pretty. You are
Gypsy Rose*, how did your words make it so?
When I was twelve, the neighbor man
Mr. Ramirez called me *pretty*—
pretty ugly. His girls were lean and dark. Their long
straight hair swayed. I'd yet to learn attraction
is more than looks; that seduction is art—exposed
shoulder, peasant blouse, lace-covered
mattress on the ground. Jangling jewelry.
Psychedelic scarves swirling like the Gypsy blood
reputed to ribbon my veins. Cousin, I know
I'm laying out clichés like shiny coins, but take one,
bite on its proof of who I am.

This want I confess:

            To steal the stage. To own the crowd,
all eyes on me not for beauty but truth. For my words
meeting a need. You understand. You learned how
people leer. You had to strip your heart clean of them
every night, so young in the mirror promising,
You will be a star. At my age,
shouldn't I be over that desire?

                You say you had no talent but hunger.
So you cultivated your voice. Sly jokes.
Taking your time to peel away a single glove.
Never baring all. Decades since Mr. Ramirez,
I do not go without rouging my cheeks.
Why choose to be vulnerable? Why admit
to wanting more? And yet in my favorite photo,

you're in shorts and bare feet under the night sky,
your long-legged four-year-old asleep in your lap.
Your eyes fish the darkness above
as if each star is an unfulfilled dream.

What is kinship, I ask you, if not desire,

                husky-throated and urgent in the night?

Cenotaph

We stood in the bright   Georgia heat

      outside the log house

           three generations   prone

                to sunburn

and stories.   My mother and her mother whispered

          the words engraved

     before us   history   on stone markers

as if reading aloud could conjure the dead.

I was only seven   but I understood

      fractions

        of blood quantum.   I was $1/32^{nd}$ Cherokee

      and the man who'd lived here   Chief John Ross

was $1/8^{th}$. I understood   we revered him

     tragic hero who lost   his wife   his home

hope of returning to his homeland   even as a corpse.   He lost all

            but his honor. I understood

my grandmother tsk-tsking   shaking her bottle-blondes

every so often   patting her waistband

        its safety-pinned house key

an amulet   against displacement

if not government atrocity.

In front of us   his house   two-storied   its long

    front porch   I wanted to explore   if only for

relief from the sun and the possibility of

a Coke machine around back.

But I understood   I needed to stand here

    with them   absorbing the whole   sorry situation.

When my mother

    was in her mother's womb,

        I was there, too, beginning.

Maybe this explains ancestral memory   how it

    clings to our cells   leaf-wet and slippery.

    Maybe this   explains my grandmother speaking as if

she was the one

who narrowly escaped

      the Trail of Tears.   Maybe this explains

her calling this house

      the old homeplace

my believing

      this man our kin.

On This Uncertain Earth

We walk expectantly among the geysers,
the land here like nothing we've known before.
We might as well be on the moon or Mars,

there's so much we can't name,
vague cues we don't recognize
until the moment they spew

hot secrets. Look how the minerals rise
and shimmer. How the mud simmers
in pastel swaths. How twilight lasts and lasts.

Now, in our room at the open window,
we lie and watch, just watch,
the cool thin air from which like magic

bats appear, scores of them,
to spin and spiral in the pine tops
because we all need to eat, and

isn't a little dancing good for the soul?
In this wilderness we've come to understand
perilous, and more than that, precarious,

and more than that, *possible*,
which is why we see now,
through the fogged gloaming,

beyond the bats and thick pines,
massive buffalo grazing, and beyond them
a lone chipmunk skittering to its burrow.

Soon it will be dark enough to see
the Milky Way, and a million stars winking
down on this yellow, bubbling earth,

down on our warm forms almost lost
among the soft spots biding their time, hungry
for something we'd rather not name.

You Are Not Who You Thought You Were

You professed to be a woman
who preferred showers,
but here you are

in a place with only a tub. It *is*
a nice tub, deep and gleaming white,
solid on four shapely dark legs,

and in considering it, you consider
the likelihood you smell
of smoke from the morning fire,

and so, in the bright mid-day
say you decide to fill the tub
plumb to the rim. Say you strip

your flannel and climb in
the water warm as a lover.
That at first you sit upright

and read your magazine,
but the water licking your legs
works its seduction, and before long

you turn to the shampoo bottle
on the windowsill and say, "Why not?"
That you edge your body first forward,

then down, down, so the water tickles
your ears and your breasts rise
like little islands in the ocean

of all you carry—your worry and hurry
and guilt (which at the moment
you feel not the least, except for

the tiniest bit of guilt that you
don't feel more guilty). Say that
after a while you say what the hell

and dip your head back and under,
then lather your graying hair,
and for the first time in years—

because showers are loud—
you hear the tiny molecular engine of suds.
Rinsing, say you look at your body—

its fine hairs and fleshy softness,
its paleness riven by dark lines
you usually think unsightly. But now,

tracing your finger along a thigh's
large vein to branches
of smaller veins, you think, *tree*.

You think, *river*. You think *I am
creation. I am mystery. Even
mysterious.* Who's to say

what elements are coursing
in those indigo veins?
And now you rise

from the water still warm
and have to resist the urge
to open the window wide

to the icy cobalt wind.
Say you drop your towel
to the floor by your clothes

and levitate to the bed,
damp and naked, and
slip between the sheets

feeling all pink and teal
and tingly. Say it feels like
it's been hours, but it's only

noon. That you like your meals
on schedule, but today
you're skipping lunch.

Say you were wrong
about this tub thing,
and you can't wait to be

wrong again, because being
wrong feels a little wicked—
lush and wicked and new.

Layers of Rich Wonder

As the Story Goes

—after Vandana Khanna

Before I was born, in a city that loves
the taste of marshmallow pies,
a sign: a Gypsy peddler, jangling

pans and fortunes, telling
me to sing, to move, to grow
ever restless of the same view.

My mother, nourished
nine months by Burger King,
on the day of my birth ate an apple

ripe as her small womb.
She would need the doctor,
curse his knife. My father,

just back from service,
all square shoulders and cleft
chin, searched for the job

that would keep him from us
hours and holidays, swearing
duty, food on the table.

These facts melt warm and familiar
as spun sugar on my tongue.
But I started longer ago, as a ship

that lost its way. As the rain
and muck of a wilderness trail.
As the shelter of a cave.

As a place called Sugar Fork,
where bats at twilight once circled
and swirled like Cherokee dancers,

where against a sky darker
than spent earth, stars float still
like manna, a hope that never fell.

Getaway

On the pop-up ad for
romantic winter retreats,
I click "No thanks, I'll stick to
my boring motel" because

one time the zipper of my parka
got stuck at my sternum,
and I was one moment cozy,
the next panicked, drowning
in nylon fiberfill, which
reminded me of a man

I once loved—a man who wouldn't,
on a beautiful night, open
the windows while we slept.
I'd wake past midnight suffocating
in the air-conditioned comfort

of his bed. So what if he rocked
a Ralph Lauren suit
like nobody's business?
I had to breathe.

Maybe I'm that woman
who wanted a fat man just for the winter.
She said she'd feed him biscuits and
thick cut bacon all season
if he'd only keep the bed warm.
But she didn't have any luck—

every man who wanted her,
wanted her year-round.

What is this urge
that makes us hold on
so tight? Even loose

and a tiny bit drunk
on a hot rum toddy, there's no way
either of us can split
a biscuit perfectly. But
if you, Honey-shucks,
will slather butter
on my slender half,
have what you will.

Take me, darling,
to the Ho-Hum Motel.
We'll have so much fun
they'll rename the place
when we're gone.

Postcards from the Cookie Jar

You can find me here most every night, it's true. Tell me your sweet
tooth doesn't nag you in the night for a bite of something sweet.

I used to fight my desire, but I'd end up pleading with my man: Bring me some
C-A-N-D-Y. As if the kids couldn't spell my favorite sweet.

Is it any wonder he took me for hot fudge cake our first date? A seduction
of chocolate laced with swirling soft serve. What a night for something sweet.

This evening the honey locust blooms by the creek as it has for ages.
Our ancestors stopped in their tracks for that scent so sweet.

You have to admit, this land's America thanks to the other side of the family—
distracted Brits, protecting that Caribbean cane. Oh, to fight for something sweet!

At Christmas I arm wrestled Aunt Will for the last piece of pecan pie.
She won. And says her diabetic comas occur to spite all that sweet.

Imagine those white men whose tongues could not form *Cullasaja*,
calling our homeland Sugar Town. Weren't they something sweet?

One old fellow called tobacco bewitching. What of the juju
of sugarcane, its slave trade, the might of something sweet?

It's in our blood, you know. We come from people who fed their kids sugar
sandwiches. Give us this day our fortified white bread, anything sweet.

Cousin, you know addiction's inherited. In the fridge, French silk pie calls.
Don't act like you don't want some. Like it's not fate to have one thin slice.

Mahaley Explains

> *By persuasion and force they have been made to retire from river to river and from mountain to mountain, until some of the tribes have become extinct and others have left but remnants to preserve for a while their once terrible name.*
> —President Andrew Jackson, in his rationale for the Indian Removal Act of 1830

How else could I have made a life?
My kin forced by soldiers from their homes,
me left alone. When the neighbor came in the night,

I braced against his rotten potato smell, the weak fire
in his eyes for drink and lust. Even then I'd known
his temper. But I saw no other way to make a life,

so I bore his ragged rhythm, pinning my mind
on the dark locust, how its pale bloom shines gold
in the day's last light. He came to me that first night

drunk and wordless, with a shudder divining
the cold way we'd be forever yoked.
Both of us alone, no other way to make a life,

I bore that Irishman child after child,
my darkness on their skin a cane flute's final note,
ever ebbing. He kept coming in the night

and named our sons for presidents, Jackson the sharpest knife
to my backbone. America, he said. Tennessee, I told
myself, I'd name our first girl. Small way to mark my life,
my only peace in the constant coming of the night.

Parable of the Pale Girl

At the end of that cloudy day in the pool,
her skin tightened, then erupted into blisters
the size of sugar pears. Laden and overripe,
they wept on her chest and back for weeks.

Every day her mother touched the hot stove of her skin
with a different salve—Noxema, Solarcaine,
some new brand of relief—and every day she passed out
from the pain. Sometimes she passed out
when only her blonde braids brushed her back.

She couldn't even bear the weight of air,
so she stayed in her room, shirtless,
alone, learning to hold her breath.
Learning to lean a certain way
when she moved. To shrink from her body.

When she finally started to heal,
her mother let a few friends visit
at the back door. Their brown eyes bugged
in their tanned faces when she
pulled back her loose robe.

They were white children, young and innocent
as they would ever be. What did they know
of suffering for your skin?

She learned it was not much comfort,
how their mouths formed a silent chorus of *ohs*.

Some Notes and Three Word Problems on Red Velvet Cake

Cousin, wasn't red velvet cake the glory
at those family Christmases? Like a red-robed chorister
it sang the call to worship from the altar of our bountiful desserts,
four layers of rich wonder, pure white boiled frosting,
a sprinkling of coconut and pecans. I find the recipe
years later in Grandmother's tattered three-ring binder.
It calls for an entire two-ounce bottle of red food coloring,
a half cup of Crisco, and a teaspoon of butter flavoring. If desired.

∞

The black nurse expertly thumps the pale crook of my arm.
I have to look away before the stick.
You've got pretty blood, she says. I'm reassured.
And skeptical. Everyone's blood isn't pretty?
Oh no. I wonder, that this could be true.

It is true that in the 1870s, the Juneteenth drink of choice
was lemonade tinted red for the blood shed by slaves.

∞

Word problem: If in the white woman's veins
there are one hundred drops of blood,
one and a half of which are from Sub-Saharan Africa,
does that knowledge change her?
Answer in complete sentences, accounting for
the likes of Dr. Walter Plecker,
who lobbied the one-drop rule into Virginia law:

any child with a single drop of black blood
categorized as black. Natives forced
to register as black. Explain why
this has been called bureaucratic genocide.

∞

It may be true that Betty and John Adams of Texas
on a trip to New York City ate the most divine
red velvet cake at the Waldorf. It is true they gave away,
at grocers, full-color recipe cards pretty enough to eat.
Their recipe, of course, called for Adams Extract
food coloring. And vanilla. And butter flavoring.

∞

Some people claim red food coloring has no flavor.
I don't believe this is true. It is true that
in 1894 the Supreme Court in Plumley vs. Massachusetts
said that food coloring serves only to delude customers.

∞

Word problem: Two cousins who've never met
walk into a cupcake shop lined with glass cases
of curvaceously topped confections, every imaginable flavor.
Calculate the likelihood both cousins will choose
red velvet. For extra credit, using genetic markers,
calculate their expected differential in skin tone.

∞

It is true I was a grown woman with children
before I realized red velvet cake is made with cocoa.

∞

My mother says the family sometimes wondered
if they had a little black blood. There was that cousin
with the nappy hair. Mostly they talked about being Cherokee.

Did you know brown sugar used to be called red sugar?

∞

Butter flavoring became popular when butter
was rationed in World War II. Thirty years later,
Grandmother was still using it in recipes.

∞

When two people, one black, one white,
discover they're a DNA match
and find each other on Facebook,
name the force that keeps them from posting
for all the world to see: *This is my cousin.*

∞

Walter Plecker is remembered as a rigid man who never
smiled. In his black and white world, how could he
ever have enjoyed a slice of Grandmother's red velvet cake?

∞

Cousin, I hope you'll come for red velvet cake.
I'll bake an all-natural version with beet juice and butter.
We'll trace our fingers on the family tree
to the grandmother we share—
Mahaley or Lucretia or one of the unnamed—
and imagine her singing from heaven to all
her children, hallelujah. With your slice of cake,
I'll offer you the gooey crumbs and frosting
that cling to the knife after the cut—messy
but my favorite part.

∞

Word problem: If you dispense two fluid ounces of red food coloring
drop by drop, how many drops will you count?
And how long will this take?

The Last Wedge of Apple Pie

In This Bright Land

Grackles arrived yesterday,
        broad chested & bold,
                strutting like sharp-eyed

soldiers to their posts
        as bullies of the birdbath,
                stalkers of the kibbled dog dish,

the cherried courtyard.
        Broom in hand this morning,
                I realize why they've come:

the first of the cicadas
        have also arrived, nymphs
                rising like the dead

from dark adolescence
        to litter the land with
                wry carcasses of birth.

I'm ashamed to say so,
        but I do not welcome
                these creatures

overturning the precedent
        of my established domain.
                Already cicadas' dry husks

cling like forsaken stories
  to the picnic table, tree trunks,
    waxwing begonias.

Now on a petal of pink
  impatiens a cicada perches,
    his body fresh & damp,

his wings newly unfurled.
  I nudge him with one finger
    & he takes flight,

first flight, I feel sure,
  as I watch him lift & zip
    through the clearing

southward, then veer
  west. From the box elder tree
    a grackle gives sudden chase,

gulps the cicada mid-air.
  I shake my broom high
    as the aproned saloon keeper

in an old western, cursing
  the dark stranger come to town.
    Sure, I could say

this is a lesson in
  biology (the life cycle),
    or economics (supply & demand),

or math (chaos theory & the butterfly effect),
  or even the law (culpability & intent).
    I could praise the cicada's

short life—flight's exhilaration,
  a quick & painless death in spring—
    as part of some perfect plan.

I could even praise the grackle,
  his euphoric, elegant strike.
    Or I could say this is our

history—someone clambering
  to rise up, someone else always
    crowding in, greedy for the plenty.

I could say this is my homeland,
  where it's hard to say when, exactly,
    all the trouble started.

Due to Chronic Inflammation

I am learning to live without sugar. Carbon, hydrogen, oxygen,
requisite as they are to life, in precise combination cause my cells
to jabber madly about a world of problems.
The body believes what it hears, believes every tiny raised alarm.
I'm desperate to be unalarmed, to take away the aches and pains
I should be too young to know. I miss cake. Cookies.
The complements to sugar: butter, egg, flour, cream, a golden
crumble of crust. These days, doesn't it seem we all have crumbs
at the corners of our mouths, moist as galloping fear?
Manchester. Aleppo. Kabul. Vegas.
An ice cream parlor. Nightclub. Baseball field.

A school full of children. Houses of worship, for God's sake.
It is hard not to fear. Terrorism, domestic incidents—
there's not much difference anymore. Wikipedia keeps a list
month by month, the number of dead and injured. What can I do
but avoid sugar substitutes and shopping malls? I want to live with
more love and less skepticism. I want to eat local honey, but there
are fewer bees. I want to read more poetry, but there are fewer
bookstores stocking fewer books. With half
its shelves in games and gadgets, the chain store in town
tells me a gathering of poets doesn't match its target

demographic. I'm learning to live in a world that runs on
metadata and compromised data and made-up data.
I'm coming to grips with a Wikipedia list that color codes
casualty levels but doesn't sum a running total. I round to
the assumption that would hurt too much. I'm learning
to live in a country where violence is never the answer,
except when it's the final answer. A country where platitudes

grow thicker than roadside weeds. #massshootingcitystrong,
you are in my prayers. I'm guilty of wondering what else I can
say. I'm learning every morning to stretch and bend. Before
the news and Twitter feed. Before my coffee. I'm fighting
every way I know for this body's flexibility, for this gray middle
between birth and death, left and right, love and oh you know it
already—I don't have it in me to hate anyone. I'm a Libra
and we're all about balance and moderation, which reminds me
of the mint ice cream quietly absorbing my freezer's stale air.
Here comes another sugar craving, but I will resist.

I'm unlearning the urge for a sugar fix like I'm unlearning
my threshold for what is acceptable, terrible, commonplace.
Tell me I don't have to unlearn hope. Sure, every stranger
could be the devil plotting our next unfathomable ruin.
On TV tonight, the lawmaker says he doesn't see
these incidents going away. I choose to imagine every stranger
as my could-be hero, rushing to my side at the sound of fire.
To the side of someone I love. This is what I have to believe
to leave the house. Because something out there has a black hole
of a soul, feeding itself first and always. It stands now at my
kitchen counter, scarfing down the last wedge of apple pie.
Willing me to lick the last morsel from its shameless lips.

"All Things Are a Darkness"

—James Dickey

Days when the house was empty,
    everyone in the fields but
        us kids, the granny-woman

        from down the way would appear
    on our porch. She smelled of soot
and sour milk but most of all

ham biscuits. We'd let her in.
    After our bellies were full,
        she'd lure us behind the door,

        show us how to charm a stream
    of milk from an ax handle.
Nights, a demon wildcat scratched

and howled on our tin roof fierce
    as a hailstorm while the worthless
        dogs shivered and whined.

        And then there were our trips home
    late from town. At sundown
sudden figures would appear

in our wagon bed—black-robed,
    faceless—weighing us down so
        the mule team frothed to pull us

                free across that haunted bridge.
        Truth can be rough or polished.
Like a hickory handle, these

tales wear a smidgen thinner,
        shinier with each use. Now
                at the old homeplace, daylight

                leaks through cracks in the clapboards
        wider than before. In each room
a bare bulb swings, opaque

as memory on a charged string,
        a corpse. Now in all the house,
                only a ratty feather tick,

                the cold cook stove. And yet
        smell of fresh biscuits. Clatter
of pail. Want is the mother

of belief. And what, my child,
        do you know of want? Of want
                for milk or second helpings?

                For new shoes, or any shoes?
        For a tight house, a good roof,
indoor plumbing, light after

darkness? To be five and wanting
        a doll, wanting your mother
                to wake from her too-long sleep,

wanting her voice to be real
and anchored to her breathing
body? I tell these stories

in hopes you tremble. In hopes
you realize: Something's coming
always for your tender soul.

They Taught Us in School to Sing of the Huddled Masses

And now we're an odd and tuneless lot,
crowded and waiting for a bus, or maybe
some crazy ride at a run-down
amusement park, tickets clutched
in sweaty hands. It's cold but we're
somewhere south. Or is it east?
Everyone's trying to avoid eye contact
or to preserve their personal space
or keep the children hushed.
None of it's working. We're over-warm.
Our coats smell of stale grease and coffee.
Someone in back lights up a cigarette,
or maybe it's smoke from a cross burning
long ago. Or yesterday. A hazy stench
first rises, then settles heavier than guilt.
A few people cough, and now someone
hands me a baby, swaddled and so small
I know she's starving, maybe even dying,
and without a thought I lift my shirt,
uncup my breast like a dove before her mouth.
My pale nipple has not nursed a child
in twenty years. The body knows.
The baby latches on, weakly at first,
then stronger, her nose so close to my flesh
I worry about her every breath.
She suckles and the milk aches its way
from deep within. I imagine it thick and gritty,
but the body knows. Little as I have,
it will be enough.

Dark strangers. I know her parents
when they come. I hand her over
with a small, soft block of something white.
Maybe it's goat cheese, or a too-obvious metaphor
for grace, or manna in new convenient packaging.
Or maybe it's an eraser, the kind draftsmen use
to fix an error, leave fragile paper clean.

On the Importance of Literature

Once, this boy told me,
he kissed a girl who
put her hand at the

back of his head & cocked
her own head back, mouth
open, eyes closed. She

even moaned a bit,
he said, but that was
all. Her fool tongue just

laid there like something
dead. I guess she'd tried
to learn how to kiss

by watching *Love Boat*
reruns instead of
reading a good book.

Me, I've always been
an avid reader.

Redoubt

I.
I'm almost ashamed to tell this
now, to confess my red-blooded
past. How after school my pulse
would race to find him. How side by side
we'd rumble through the parking lot,
then rev and tease our engines
to a frenzy at every stoplight
into town. His blue GTO,
my dark green Mustang—

the Fastback caught his eye before
my long blonde hair. My hips.
On Broad Street we'd gun it
to Kroger, where he bagged groceries
and bought M&Ms for my mother,
an offering at our door. All these years later

I remember most our parking.
Dark country roads, gravel shoulders,
Feels So Right playing low. That soft
dashboard glow. Windows obscured by
lust and a Confederate flag which
I know sounds redneck or worse,

but I liked his blue jean jacket.
Rough-with-stubble jawline. Scent
of soap and drugstore aftershave.
How he seemed less boy than man. I liked
how he kissed, how I kissed him back,

the playful push and pull of it all. I liked him
till the day he broke the news: *I ain't wearing
no monkey suit to prom.* Righteous

children raised in Redoubt Brannan's
shadows, we stonewalled in silence
Lincoln himself couldn't have healed.
What did I expect from a boy
even the teachers called Rebel?
What did he expect from a girl
who always called him by his real name?

II.
When first I heard the word, I was eight or nine,
standing ill at ease in a cedar-stubbed field
not two miles from our three-bedroom ranch,
fretting about seed ticks, the sun bearing down

relentless as past mistakes. A stone-voiced
park ranger told the tale I already knew: hand-to-hand
combat, young brother against brother, the Stones River
red with blood. Then Union occupation, an earthen
fort, walls ten feet high, span a mile. And within
the fort, that word—

redoubt. A fort within a fort, but nothing
like Fort Nashborough, another field trip,
another era, its walls of wooden poles uniform,
round, predictable. *That* was a fort. This was nothing
but a hill, given over to tall grass and brush.
And, I realize now, to the willful years.

III.

*Walk Where Civil War Soldiers Fought
and Died.* Part of me's embarrassed to admit
those billboard words make me cringe, embarrassed
to admit I'm so un-American I believe
marketing's a kind of war that aims to take
every last cause as prisoner. Or maybe
my trouble's with a message too simple
for a history I can't reconcile—in this place,
at that time, how does *hero* ever follow
the word *hometown*? But it does, and I am
divided country: Proud for my forebears
who defended their homes. Uneasy
for my newfound black cousins. Bitter
for my native ancestors driven from their land.
Hasn't death and suffering of all
these people made this earth sacred?
I imagine a more sensational sign:
See Cemetery That Banned Local Soldiers.
Or metaphorical: *Hike Stone Outcroppings
Symbolic of Issues We Stumble on Today.*
After all, CNN's come to town to report
a one-hour special on construction of a new mosque—
the latest thing dividing us.

IV.

What's past is prologue, Shakespeare said, but here
in the South the past is a teenager—sultry and sullen,
shampooed and Sunday-schooled, hopped in the hot backseat
with progress any chance she gets. They're going at it
now, all tongue and touch, each with an eye peeled for who might see.
The pressure's too much. Soon they'll argue.

She'll get out, slam the car door, straighten her clothes,
stride back to town. Despite the dark, she'll see everything's
changed—even the streets and their names. Two lanes
under five, Big Lots where Kroger used to be, Kroger
in five, six, who knows how many locations. Identical
rooflines flank the highway like soldiers, at the ready
to sacrifice any uniqueness lingering on this flat piece
of Tennessee. It's all too different, yet all too same.
She thinks she might call him in the morning, ask
if he misses the redoubts. Maybe they can start again,
agree on that one thing. After all, there's always
something to defend. Even the claim that all is lost.

My Zinnias Grow Like Good Intentions

I apologize as I stand before them this morning, garden shears in hand. Because I planted their seed in diminished sun, the only sun in our shaded yard. Because they grow thick and misshapen, racing across earth toward the two o'clock light, curving and breaking for the brittle ceiling of my expectations. Because my assumptions have been so wrong. How they think. How they feel. How they synthesize their wisdom into endless blooms. Because summer's blazed relentless, our discontent settling like the humid air. Because men arrived with weapons. Because a car can be a weapon. Because the violence of politics. Because the politics of violence.

This world careens every moment in drastic misdirections of belief. And aren't we all to blame? I've made the mistake of speaking softly; of speaking too little; of speaking too much. The zinnias have stood night after night bearing the weight of their heavy heads. They face another frenzied day of sweat bees, duskywings, hummingbirds. And now they know I've come again to ask more: To bleed not. To endure the pain. To turn that pain into keeping on. To grow across the whole damn yard to spite me. Imperfect in the half-light. Furious in their vivid hope.

The Biggest Buttercream Rose

Unlike Emily's

Her hope has teeth. It's not some flighty, feathered
thing that chirps and springs from branch to sill
within her soul. It is, instead, a wild
and rowdy beast that crashes fencerow, charges
through the woods of her incessant wants:
A better job, a bigger house, another
pair of shoes. An artful life, and children—
with no man, perhaps. Or with more than one.

A beast so large cannot be sated long.
It stalks her next outlandish dream and, catching
scent, throws its heavy weight from side to fickle
side, trampling tender violets, muddy jags
to nowhere. Jilted, she seeks in the brambles
a solitary wren to follow home.

I confess I've never been completely satisfied

—in my kitchen, although I love
its butterscotch walls and copper spoons,
its pressed glass jars of sugar,
the ragged sound of their rusting screw-top lids.

The room is too small.
I've tried on the words
cozy, intimate. Found the fit
revelatory. How padded my ribs have become.

Bread and butter, cake and frosting—
I confess these excesses,
but if you asked,
I have some shame.

I confess to affairs of the heart,
loving first one room,
then another, for the light,
for the sloping honey-colored floors.

I confess to an eye that roams, an addiction
for odd dishes and glass rabbits,
for sweetened coffee and books.
Of course books. And anyone who reads.

It's true you still bring me chocolate.
But don't you miss our desire
rattling the saucers on their shelves?
I've cried for such want, tears like Karo syrup.

Unlike Emily's

Her hope has teeth. It's not some flighty, feathered
thing that chirps and springs from branch to sill
within her soul. It is, instead, a wild
and rowdy beast that crashes fencerow, charges
through the woods of her incessant wants:
A better job, a bigger house, another
pair of shoes. An artful life, and children—
with no man, perhaps. Or with more than one.

A beast so large cannot be sated long.
It stalks her next outlandish dream and, catching
scent, throws its heavy weight from side to fickle
side, trampling tender violets, muddy jags
to nowhere. Jilted, she seeks in the brambles
a solitary wren to follow home.

I confess I've never been completely satisfied

—in my kitchen, although I love
its butterscotch walls and copper spoons,
its pressed glass jars of sugar,
the ragged sound of their rusting screw-top lids.

The room is too small.
I've tried on the words
cozy, intimate. Found the fit
revelatory. How padded my ribs have become.

Bread and butter, cake and frosting—
I confess these excesses,
but if you asked,
I have some shame.

I confess to affairs of the heart,
loving first one room,
then another, for the light,
for the sloping honey-colored floors.

I confess to an eye that roams, an addiction
for odd dishes and glass rabbits,
for sweetened coffee and books.
Of course books. And anyone who reads.

It's true you still bring me chocolate.
But don't you miss our desire
rattling the saucers on their shelves?
I've cried for such want, tears like Karo syrup.

White is distance, a mountain, a blinding buzz of bees.
I've become a woman who adds sugar to beans.
I've crashed parties for the cake's biggest buttercream rose.
I've taken it all at once in my mouth.

"We Climb onto the Motorcycle of Sleep"

—Jane Gentry

Jane, I love that image—
you holding tight to him,
your white scarf shimmering
in the night wind. It's how I sleep
with my man, too. But Jane,
can I ask about that roar
you mention? Has it grown
more noticeable through the years?
As your irresistible bad boy
freewheels through starry space,
does he sound like a Honda Goldwing?
A Kawasaki? A Harley?

My man's like a Harley,
a vintage model that rumbles
louder with every revolution
of engine and Earth. A problem
with the carburetor, I suspect.
Why, he sputters and gasps
and even backfires once in a while,
so deafening sometimes
I'm tempted to adjust the choke

right there in the darkness. I confess
I've thought how much quieter
a new model would be. But then
we circle back into the morning
glint of day bright as chrome:

those old plugs still spark,
that engine still cranks,
and despite the dents, pings, and misses,
the ride's still smooth
as sheets on the fresh-made bed
before we take the night
on one more thunderous spin.

Questions from the Women for Dorothy, Wife of Richard Cantrell, Before the Grand Jury for Masking in Men's Clothes and Dancing at Nine O'Clock at Night, 1703

   1.
Silk waistcoat,
or wool?

   2.
Are late nights a matter of
your constitution? How often
do you leave your chamber
to wander the silent house? In thin light
lean over your child and watch
the soft metronome of his chest?

   3.
When your husband first saw you
in gentleman's breeches,
where did his eyes linger?
At your slender hips,
bare of their usual hoops?
Or at the curve
of your stockinged calf?

   4.
Have you welcomed always
his wind-chapped lips
at your clavicle?
Do his attentions

still make you sing
soprano afternoons?

5.
Your gentleman's suit
brilliant as the autumn hills—
have you ever believed
it's the color of sin?

6.
Did the very anticipation
of the masquerade
increase your ardor
for your husband
of all these years?
Would you claim the same
for him?

7.
The lightness
of your dance step—
is it ballast
for those dark days
after infant Mary passed?
Or does it come from
your mother, herself
a woman prone to society?

8.
Did you tremble,
dancing in the arms
of another so masked?

9.
Was marrying out of church
your first step toward
debauchery?

10.
Do you truly believe your husband,
who spends his days
permeating clay with water,
waiting for the kiln's hot
flourish, and building fair
Philadelphia block by block,
has never had the urge
to mold you
like one of his bricks?

11.
Was it your husband
or another
who whispered
wicked in your ear?
And did you not
take some measure of delight
in being named so?

12.
This offense that brings you before the court
of wigged men shaking
their heads in fashionable curls—
would you do it again?

Her First Husband Was a Carpenter

Some nights she'd call for him to pour the water
down her spine, then let him stay as rising
from the tub she bloomed, pale pink and Ivory-
scrubbed. He'd dab the glisten from her skin,
the towel all sunshined stiff with smell of bleach
and pine. Inhale her warmth. Gardenia.

Too long in water, though, her fingers shriveled,
response involuntary as breath,
as perspiration, as the double-drub
of illicit love pounding in her heart.

When does the blossom ever choose the bee?

Long nights after, the memory cleaved to her—
how his rough fingers glossed her knobby truss
of spine. Like a board he tested for splinters.

Salve of Spun Honey

We're Young and This Is the Beginning

Evening we walk a garden of amethyst
marvels—structures and steel, pylons
and progress, burst-blossoms of light.
Between skyscrapers we gather close
our coats as steam swoops
from the underground, nearby
the scent of coffee and yeast
almost enough to tempt our course.

Earlier, I took your hand for the first time,
inked on your palm an address.
This is where I want us to go, that word, *us,*
hanging like the full moon in tonight's dark
blue note of sky. Now, blocks away, sirens.
A woman pilfers a trashcan for dinner.
A man dead-walks into stopped traffic,
palms high. As if it will ease the desperation,
you reach for my hand. Or do I reach
for yours? We are new and believe
we need an excuse to touch.

Above us, rows and rows of windows,
like diamonds in a jeweler's case, flash
with a thousand shiny promises. Flash
like a fevered undoing of buttons and cuffs.

At an open door we find our belonging—
a woman in jazz club shadow-smoke,
her mouth at the mic a bloom of orchid,

her voice a plume of pleasure and truth.
She sings our fortune.

Later, the streets all but empty, we walk
and walk and my shoes rub blisters but
we're hand in hand—what's a little pain?
Beside us the topaz river glints.

The Assistant Marshal Makes
an Error in Judgment

> —*from the Ninth United States Census, June 18, 1870,*
> *Macon County, North Carolina*

Even though he has read and reread
best he can the instructions
sent direct from Washington;

even though he employs
a sturdy portable inkstand,
quality ink he blots dry
with unpracticed diligence
on strictly confidential,
wide white sheets;

even though important scientific
results depend upon his questionable
Rs and too-short Ls, tedious
recording of Name, Age, Occupation,
and Color;

Assistant Marshal J.T. Reeves, who some call
carpetbagger, now sits amiably on the porch
with one Willis Guy, farmer, age 59,
and reads back to Mr. Guy
all he has written, so mistakes may be
corrected on the spot. The marshal is not
from around these parts, and Mr. Guy,

previously known as
Mulatto, previous to that known as

Free Colored Person, if asked would claim
Catawba, Cherokee, even the dark Porterghee,
but figures it best to keep his silence
at the government man's ditto of Column 6. Like that,
Mr. Guy and all his kin become
White. Mr. Guy would admit he isn't
as good at letters as his children,
but squinting sideways at the marshal's ledger,
he knows the unmistakable difference between W and M.

With a Thousand-Tongued Hunger

Sunset at our campsite, and you kneel,
faith healer to feeble embers of fire.
Through damp wood your breath rises
a small miracle of enough—
flame to cook our supper,
light to stave the darkness,
heat to warm our hands.
But our backs chill.

This reminds us of happiness—
one turn, the warmth gone.
How often is the forecast wrong?
Clearing skies portend colder ground
beneath our tent tonight. For all we plan,
life's more paradox than perfection.
You tell me it's possible to hold
at once great sorrow and joy,

that one does not cancel the other
on some cosmic ledger of accounts.
In the balance of time I may never
move as easily as you,
ahead on the overgrown path.
But I savor all you notice,
the names you know:
trillium, warbler, brim.

You soothe-talk a small fish
as you unhook and toss him back
to his shining home. For this I want to rise

to my feet and clap. Why not
honor compassion with ovation?
Why not too often say *love*?
At the choppy lakeshore,
water gulps stones. *This this this*.

We know that desire, that frenzy,
but today we sun on a slab of stone,
lizards blinking. The sinkhole behind us
could yawn wider anytime. We study
a rock under the water's surface.
Flat as a palm, marked by a lifeline
some might call jagged. We wade out
ankle-deep, a kind of blessing.

Between Past and Present
I Never Moved So Freely

A teenage recruit for living history
that summer at the antebellum home

                                                         in long skirt
                                                       and petticoat

I followed my script
without question,

                                         a true Southern belle,

I imagined,

                                              greeting and
                                            charming guests

with facts and anecdotes:

We're now standing (please,
move all the way into the room)
in the oldest part of the house,
furnished as it might have appeared
in the early 1860s. Imagine

                                                a young lady
                                      playing the harpsichord

(sir, I must ask you
not to touch) original
to the house,

                                                  entertaining
                                          family and visitors

such as yourselves

                                                  before dinner,
                                         the table set with

this exact

                                                Haviland china

         all the way from France,
      afterward the gentlemen retiring
        to the library and cigars,
        the ladies to the parlor,

note the low doorknobs—
people were shorter back then.

Here in the master's
chamber, be sure to see

           the exquisite
      trapunto coverlet, hand-wrought
        quatrefoil bedposts.

Yes, they slept
propped up! Imagine

        the mosquitoes in summer,
         no window screens.

Imagine

           the servants

my script called them
servants

     on the steep back stairs, wearing down
       the hard poplar treads.

Imagine

        the mansion's mistress,
       a key to the sugar chest
       tucked at her delicate,
        hammering heart.

Pull back the lace curtain
(it's alright to touch) and picture

                                        soldiers on the lawn,
                                the occupation well underway.

Never did I say
imagine

                                acres of cotton so endless.
                                                      Never
did I think
to say

                                                    imagine
                                                welted backs,

                                                    fingers,
                                        how they would bleed.
unfree

"Let Us Suffer Our Radiance"

—Cecilia Woloch

In a brilliant clash of atoms,
I dreamt, the world was ending

and somehow you and I
were wombed in the dim

chances of a limestone cave.
For a while it wasn't so bad—

the dank darkness we held at bay
with a half-life of batteries,

the hunger we staved
with stockpiled cans of soup—

but all I wanted was fresh air,
and when I couldn't have that

all I wanted was to accept
a pre-apocalypse invitation

to a baby shower,
but there were no phones

and likely no babies
gleaming and new, so I thought

at least I can take comfort
in reading, in the failing light

coaxing words like little wild animals
from the dusky forest of pages,

but in the rush to the cave,
I'd left my books behind.

Finally all I could do was
lie with you

and stroke your fingers
and speak softly

of goose down pillows
and cream in our coffee

and how I used to squint in the morning sun
so bright at the kitchen window,

and I couldn't bear to say it aloud,
but all I wanted was for you to know

that if you should leave this dying earth first,
I would finger-trace your name in limestone

until there was dust,
and the dust remembered.

I'd find a way to wash your body
till it glistened like all our years.

Fall Sanctuary

—after Jeff Hardin

I slept in a room that glowed with fireflies,
though it was late autumn on a frosty bluff
high above Lost Cove. The room was a salve
of spun honey and light, and a hundred
little windowpanes gauzed with tranquility.

In a wide bed I slept alone, surrounded
by pillows and books, by poets I love.
In the night I lit a candle and a tiny string of lights
against the darkness. They were a comfort.
So was the darkness.

Outside I found an astonishment of stars,
a clear sky, spangled and deep.
How long had it been since I'd seen the stars?

This is how I fell asleep: my skin on soft cotton,
my body awaiting the gentle touch of fireflies,
their silent sparks. This is how I awoke:
unencumbered and enthralled, the early sun
casting over the mountain autumn into my room,
casting through the morning chill a stained-glass chapel,

                    a splendor of stillness, stirring.

In the Secret Hour of Life's Midday

> *For in the secret hour of life's midday the parabola*
> *is reversed, death is born.*
> —Carl Jung

You'd think we'd be road-weary,
but oh the clear blue sky,

the just-right chill,
these early morning Virginia

hills veiled with fog.
Look at the glint of garnet

and gold leaves, dapple of sun
and shadow, the fullness

of the pumpkin, the lavish curve
of the gooseneck gourd.

Did you notice the modest stones
studding the hillside graveyard

we passed? We too are bound
for the cold and reluctant bones

of winter, but now, because
life is ever closer to death, now,

because this death before us is so alive,
now this beauty takes our breath

at every bend in the road and I
want to open my shirt

and lean out the window
bare-breasted in the wind,

in this rush of loveliness.
I want to shout to the earth

take me, take me now.

As I Already Said, Sugar

When the Watched Pot Boils

You know time is getting by,
and you try to remember
all she told you:

Use both dark meat and white.
Save bone and skin and gristle
for the cat. Roll the dough thin
as a paper sack. Slice it into strips
no wider than your thumb.
You'd give up sweets for a month
to hold again her wood-handled knife,
its old blade so often sharpened
it was almost gone.

You think of these things
as you stand at the stove,
the kettle's broth rolling.
Think of the stories she told.
That time a door-to-door peddler
tried to snatch her youngest.
That hot night she and her lover
broke every dish in the house.
That Sunday the kids ate
their own pet rooster for lunch.
Reminding you,
chicken and dumplings need
plenty of salt. You taste

that name passed down to her,
Tennessee,

and she is with you,
barefoot, stirring the pot,
one eyebrow raised.
That hard T, that soft S,
the irony she was born
in Georgia and lies now
all too soon, in Alabama soil.

Some things are never right.
Some things are not better with time.
But maybe her name was perfect.
After all, how many of the stories
she told had a happy ending?

There's a God of False Starts and Tragic Mistakes

A friend says she can't
embrace, can't speak
another word about
this small finality—
at her cabin, mostly empty
for the winter, bluebirds
flew down the stovepipe
and couldn't get back out.
Twice. The first time

she rescued them, but
this time she was too late.
I think of a man who planned
to come back from the dead
as an owl and wonder

if those poor birds, caught
in her cold wood stove,
had a previous life, or if
they're headed to another
life now. Well, sure they are—
at least in the form of carbon
and dust. I'm no mystic,
but someone once said
that the lives we don't choose
still leave their marks upon us.

Once I wanted to be a pilot,
and I learned to fly a small plane

over the rolling hills of home.
But every time you take off,
you must also land. I was never
good at landings. So then

I wanted to be a musician,
and I learned to sing and play
a small guitar. But music depends
on breath, and I haven't always
been good at breathing. Still,

I will go to my grave wanting
to fly and sing like a bird.
Is it such a weakness
to come to a cold end
trapped in hope?

Praise those birds
as you found them,
I tell my friend—
against dull ash,
a bright, persistent blue.

This Relic

The tree man splits the morning's silence.

> His lumbering trucks and straight-backed crew
> have come to take the backyard
> honey locust, namesake of my ancestral home—
> Cullasaja, meaning honey locust place.
>
> The tree is dying. Maybe it knows
> it's destined for extinction—
> low sharp thorns and long black pods
> only a mastodon could chew.
>
> At my kitchen window I stand watching,
> an accessory to fact after fact
> I remind myself: The tree
> is a danger. The tree could fall
> on the house, the neighbor's car,
> any unguarded mortal. But does the tree
> deserve death? My teeth grind
> a honeycrisp apple. Its sweet flesh
> swells mid-swallow.

The lift is called a cherry picker,

> meaning aerial work platform, meaning
> common phrases fall sometimes short of
> the images they conjure.
>
> Soon the tree man's tree-top high
> as if he's a god, bringing judgment

    on first one limb, then another.
    While he wields one-handed a chainsaw
    like a great buzzing bassoon,
    his free hand directs large logs
    to a deep bass vibrato on the ground.

The heart, of course, is a muscle,

    meaning mine contracts with each earth-shaking thud.

    Is the throat also a muscle? I wonder,
    constricting at the thought
    of crushed nests, lost stashes of acorns.

    Tender limbs the tree man
    now shaves quick as whiskers
    on a grizzled Irishman named Culligan,
    descendant of Colgan, derived from *coll*, meaning
    hazel tree, meaning I come from many different
    bloodlines, and people are inseparable
    from nature.

A soft heart is often said to be a weakness,

    and now we see inside
    the reason the tree was dying,
    on the crosscut a core of crimson—
    disease, the tree man says—but I see

    a tattoo roughly the shape of a bird
    and think of Sacagawea,
    meaning bird-woman,
    or perhaps boat-puller, meaning

       historians and Shoshone argue ceaselessly
       how to pronounce her name, meaning
       aren't all of us always reckoning our next step,
       and who will be brave enough to lead the way?

Somewhere in time I once stood at the mouth

       of a wizened Lakota chief as he declared
       his native language must not die.

       I thought I heard the flat-topped hills moan.

Sacagawea. Culligan. Cullasaja. Not names

       the linguists put together, but music
       of syllables, notes of our ever-thirsty throats, faint
       markings on my DNA. I want to find the words to parse

Manifest Destiny, connection, loss. But all I know is this:

       Now the workers trod ankle-high grass,
       blood-drops of tiny wild berries.
       Now they feed timber to the wood chipper
       that rips and roars like a fabled giant
       wild-eyed with greed. It is ugly. And yet
       wood shavings spew
       like water from a fountain.
       And yet this death smells sweet.

Love Me Anyway

—with a line from Cecilia Woloch's "Fireflies"

And these are my vices:

    Envy, sloth, sugar   butter, salt, sweet

      wine in screw-top bottles, cheap

   sparkly jewelry and saying yes   to every good cause

      and even some lost ones.

And how I dance gracelessly

                and abandon novels too easily

  after the first climax   and drift from my sentences

  especially in the bleary mornings

     after late nights strumming

song after song   till my fingertips ache.

And how I'm not bold enough

          to always speak for all that's right

  not faithful enough   to believe in the power of prayer

                    more than I believe in

            the curve of my hips because

as I already said: Sugar.

Your lips. Your voice.   The way my insides quicken.

How even though it irks you

            I never close the pantry door

the packages perched inside   bright birds that sing

        our paradise, and I'm hungry

                            always hungry for more.

Voice

When she'd hand the rope to me,
she could've said, Here, jump
on out of my way—

I've got laundry to hang,
supper to cook, a shirt to mend,
this book I want to read.

She'd already taught me
Miz Mary Mac, those silver buttons,
all the other singsong rhymes.

Now she was teaching me
about metaphor, otherwise known as
pretend. She could've said, Here,

this is a snake—pretend
it wants to bite you, but
she was not teaching me to fear.

She could've said, Here,
find someone to play tug-of-war,
but she was not teaching me

to require the presence
of others. She could've said,
Here, this is how you make

a noose, but she was not
teaching me violence
or hatred. No,

my mother handed me
one end of that rope
secured in a stiff knot

and said, Here,
this is a microphone.
What can you sing?

We Come Undone

Because we fail to measure twice,
cut once. Because the floor beneath us
threatens to give way. Water drips.
Hardwood warps. Finish and shine

wear thin. In the week before spring,
two baby rabbits frozen in the yard.
There's so much we can't explain.
A machine levels mountains.

The government oils the machine.
Bullets ricochet through vital
strangers. We forget to listen,
bring the tickets, check the ingredients,

breathe. Because long ago I veered from
the curve of your innocent cheek.
Because you're caught in the traffic jam
of my heart. Because the street names keep

changing. Construction is delayed.
We've only just realized the detour
is the scenic route. And now in my throat
a lump persists. The ultrasound lights up

unknowns. Someday, the widowmaker
will cleave us, leave one of us
lamenting artery's plaque, sweetgum's
deadwood. Let us never mind.

Today we thrive. Today a warm
hillside slopes to the lake. Today
our blanket blooms showy
and wild beneath budding oak.

The moist soil thirsts and the constant
geese call. Today we are that call
across the charged heavens, all joy
and ache and home.

So Long to the Good Old Moon

—Life *magazine headline, July 4, 1969*

When I was young, I wanted to go to the moon
    but I've only made it to Milwaukee,
        which is to say I have learned

        about adjusting expectations.
    When I was young I planned to move
to the big city, any big city,

but my hometown grew and grew
    in a labyrinth of commerce around me,
        which is to say only certain bodies at rest

        tend to stay at rest, not to mention
    good urban planning is a must. When I was young,
I was going to drive a Porsche 944 flat on the floor

but I've been all four-door sedans and minivans
        full of kids   I was not planning
            and a husband   I was not planning

        the latter of whom came into my life
    wearing plaid pants which I was
definitely   not   planning.

Love is the unbalanced force
    unnamed in Newton's first law
        and I learned early on:

        one, to accept people as they are
    even if they have no fashion sense; and two,
planning will only take you so far, but love—

love will take you everywhere, even
    to Milwaukee in winter, which is to say
        although I reserve the right to complain

    we do what we have to do. Older now,
I take uncommon pleasure simply anticipating
an afternoon cappuccino

from a powdered mix, which is to say life
    is improbable, and if you look you'll find a galaxy
        in your cup, perfect and round and spinning.

Acknowledgments

Grateful acknowledgment is made to the editors of the following publications in which these poems first appeared, sometimes in slightly different versions.

APIARY: "They Taught Us in School to Sing of the Huddled Masses"

As It Ought to Be Magazine: "The Assistant Marshal Makes an Error in Judgment," "Untold Story," "When the Watched Pot Boils"

Ascent: "So Long to the Good Old Moon"

Broad River Review: "We Come Undone"

Crannóg Magazine: "Love Me Anyway"

Forage: "As the Story Goes"

The Heartland Review: "All Things Are a Darkness"

Helen: "He Drove a Four-Door Chevy, Nothing Sexy, But I'd Been Thinking of His Mouth for Weeks"

James Dickey Review: "Between Past and Present I Never Moved So Freely"

Kissing Dynamite: "My Zinnias Grow Like Good Intentions"

Mothers Always Write: "Voice" (published as "First Muse")

the museum of americana: "Questions from the Women for Dorothy, Wife of Richard Cantrell, Before the Grand Jury for Masking in Men's Clothes and Dancing at Nine O'Clock at Night, 1703"

Number One: "In the Secret Hour of Life's Midday"

Parks and Points: "On This Uncertain Earth"

Passager: "Her First Husband Was a Carpenter"

Sheila-Na-Gig online: "I confess I've never been completely satisfied," "You Are Not Who You Thought You Were"

Southern Women's Review: "We Climb onto the Motorcycle of Sleep"

Stirring: "Postcards from the Cookie Jar"

2 Elizabeths: "Dear Reader"

Typishly: "Getaway"

The Wild Word: "There's a God of False Starts and Tragic Mistakes"

Words Dance: "We're Young and This Is the Beginning"

"Still Won't Marry" was published in *Don't Forget This Song: Four Writers Celebrate the Carter Family and Other Roots Musicians* by Maggi Vaughn, Carole Knuth, Kory Wells, and Kelsey Wells (Bell Buckle Press, 2011).

"Unlike Emily's" was published in *Journey to Crone*, ed. S. Philip (Chuffed Buff Books, 2013).

"So Long to the Good Old Moon" was reprinted in *Collage: A Journal of Creative Expression*, and won the fall 2018 Martha Hixon Creative Expression Award for Poetry.

"So Long to the Good Old Moon" and "With a Thousand-Tongued Hunger" were reprinted in *In God's Hand*, Ed. Rosemary Royston (Writers of Grace Evangelical Lutheran Church, Oak Ridge, TN, 2017).

"We Climb onto the Motorcycle of Sleep" was reprinted in *Time and Tradition: A Poetry Anthology*, ed. Philip M. Mathis (Twin Oaks Press, 2011).

"We're Young and This Is the Beginning" was reprinted in
 Collage: A Journal of Creative Expression.

"With a Thousand-Tongued Hunger" was the 2016 HeartWood Broadside Series winner.

I am grateful to a generous community of writers who enrich my life with exchanges, inspiration, advice, and opportunities. Special thanks to poets Bryanna Licciardi and Susan Martinello and novelist Jennie Fields for their friendship, feedback, and sustained engagement with the poems in this book. Thanks also to the Poetry in the Boro community and to my mentors and teachers, Darnell Arnoult, Bill Brown, and Jeff Hardin.

Several poems in this book arose from a nine-week writing exchange with Gloria Ballard. I am indebted to Gloria for patiently helping me gain a better understanding of the African American experience and for being a fellow bridge builder and longtime friend.

Although it has ceased operation, I also owe a debt of gratitude to Rivendell Writers' Colony, where many of these poems first came into being, and to Sandy Coomer for leading me there.

Finally, thanks to Diane Lockward at Terrapin for the encouragement she sent when she rejected the first version of *Sugar Fix*. One hopeful sentence fueled a year of revision and led to a most thrilling *yes*.

About the Author

Kory Wells is the author of *Heaven Was the Moon*, a poetry chapbook from March Street Press (2009). Her writing has appeared in numerous publications, including the *James Dickey Review*, *Ruminate*, *Stirring*, and *The Southern Poetry Anthology*. She also performs her poetry on the album *Decent Pan of Cornbread*, a collaboration with her daughter, folk musician Kelsey Wells.

A seventh generation Tennessean, Kory worked in software development before leaving that career to focus on her creative life. In 2017 she was selected as the inaugural Poet Laureate of Murfreesboro, Tennessee. She is founder and manager of Poetry in the Boro, a reading and open mic series, and is active as an arts advocate, teaching artist, and storyteller. She is also a mentor with the low-residency program MTSU Write and a board member of the Rockvale Writers' Colony.

Sugar Fix is her first full-length collection.

www.korywells.com

About the Author

Kory Wells is the author of *Heaven Was the Moon*, a poetry chapbook from March Street Press (2009). Her writing has appeared in numerous publications, including the *James Dickey Review*, *Ruminate*, *Stirring*, and *The Southern Poetry Anthology*. She also performs her poetry on the album *Decent Pan of Cornbread*, a collaboration with her daughter, folk musician Kelsey Wells.

A seventh generation Tennessean, Kory worked in software development before leaving that career to focus on her creative life. In 2017 she was selected as the inaugural Poet Laureate of Murfreesboro, Tennessee. She is founder and manager of Poetry in the Boro, a reading and open mic series, and is active as an arts advocate, teaching artist, and storyteller. She is also a mentor with the low-residency program MTSU Write and a board member of the Rockvale Writers' Colony.

Sugar Fix is her first full-length collection.

www.korywells.com

www.ingramcontent.com/pod-product-compliance
Lightning Source LLC
Chambersburg PA
CBHW020144130526
44591CB00030B/199